DAYS THAT CHANGED THE WORLD

THE FREEING OF
NELSON MANDELA

Simon Beecroft

ticktock
M E D I A

Copyright © ticktock Entertainment Ltd 2003
First published in Great Britain in 2003 by ticktock Media Ltd.,
Unit 2, Orchard Business Centre, North Farm Road, Tunbridge Wells, Kent, TN2 3XF
ISBN 1 86007 423 5 pbk
ISBN 1 86007 430 8 hbk
Printed in Taiwan
A CIP catalogue record for this book is available from the British Library.

CONTENTS

INTRODUCTION

On Sunday February 11th, 1990, Nelson Mandela was released from prison after more than 27 years behind bars. The eyes of the world were on this frail, white-haired man who had become a symbol of freedom for South Africans and millions of others around the world. All his adult life, Nelson Mandela had struggled for equality between South Africa's black and white populations, and for an end to the system of racial segregation called apartheid. This struggle cost him his freedom, but not his dream, and after his release, Mandela became South Africa's first black president. Today, even though Mandela has handed power over to Thabo Mbeki, he remains an icon of tolerance and humanity.

Throughout the apartheid regime, the treatment of blacks by the police was often harsh and brutal.

Nelson Mandela was born on July 18th, 1918, in a village in a region of South Africa called Transkei. He was born into a royal family of the Tembu, a Xhosa-speaking tribe. In the Xhosa language, his

Prior to his arrest, Mandela was a prominent lawyer in Johannesburg. (Image by Jurgen Schadeberg)

By 1948, the organization had come to dominate the ANC itself, and in 1950, Mandela became president of the Youth League.

For all of the 20th century, the beautiful South African countryside (above) was scarred by decades of civil unrest.

Even after his retirement, Nelson Mandela has remained influential in world affairs.

birth name, Rolihlahla, means 'stirring up trouble'. Mandela was educated at Fort Hare University, from which he was expelled in 1940. He returned home, but ran away to Johannesburg to avoid an arranged marriage. He eventually obtained a law degree from the University of South Africa. Helped by Walter Sisulu, Mandela and his friend Oliver Tambo set up South Africa's first black law firm. In 1944, frustrated at the lack of impact the African National Congress (ANC) was having on the white government, the group formed the African National Congress Youth League.

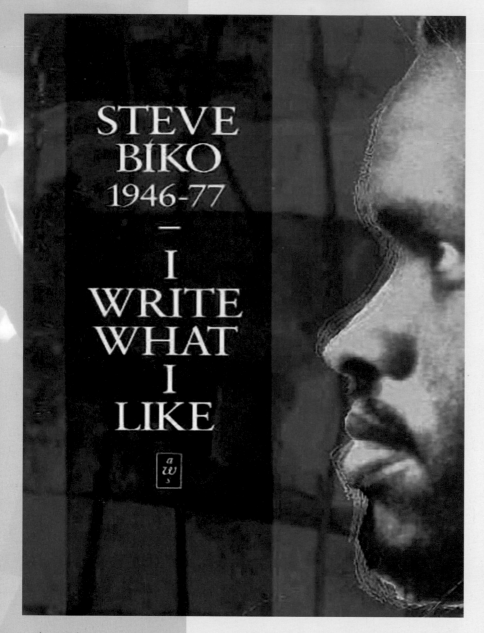

STEVE
BIKO
1946-77
–
I
WRITE
WHAT
I
LIKE

The struggle against apartheid was taken up by Steve Biko and the Black Consciousness movement in the 1970s.

'In my country we go to prison first and then become President.'

Nelson Mandela

and treason and was sentenced to life imprisonment.

While Mandela was in prison, his supporters continued the struggle on his behalf. In the 1970s, the Black Consciousness movement – led by Steve Biko – took up the cause, urging blacks to have pride in their own identity. Then, in the 1980s, an organization called the United Democratic Front (UDF) launched a national campaign called 'Release Mandela'. With an outbreak of shocking violence in the 1980s, and the election of President FW de Klerk, the political leadership in South Africa also realised that things would have to change.

In 1960, the government banned the ANC after the Sharpeville Massacre, in which 69 protestors were shot down by police. Mandela felt compelled to turn away from peaceful protest to engage in more robust opposition. In 1964, he was found guilty of carrying out acts of sabotage

By the end of the decade, the South African government had begun negotiating Mandela's release, with the latter determining the terms of his freedom. Then, on February

11th, Nelson Mandela was finally released to cheering crowds.

Mandela's release marked the beginning of a new chapter for South Africa. While de Klerk's government announced that it would gradually phase out apartheid, Mandela realised how impatient the people of South Africa had become and forced de Klerk to increase the pace of change. In 1994, the first universal elections were held, and Mandela was elected as the first black president of South Africa. In 1999, Nelson Mandela retired, but he still plays an active role in the affairs of his country. And while South Africa still faces many challenges ahead, the role Mandela played in destroying the hated system of apartheid will never be forgotten by its people.

South Africa lies at the bottom of the continent. It is rich in gold and diamonds, which meant it was of great importance to white settlers in the 19th and 20th centuries.

Nelson Mandela has been married three times, and has 45 children and grandchildren.

The Dutch were the first Europeans to arrive in South Africa. The Dutch East India Trading Company (centre) used its fine fleet to take goods in and out of Africa.

This Bantu boy is learning traditional hunting techniques. The Bantus have been in South Africa for hundreds of years.

South Africa is a country with a troubled history. Since the first European contact in the 15th century, Dutch and British adventurers fought to control this vast land. This led to a political situation in which, for most of the 20th century, South Africa was ruled by a white minority. It was this long ingrained tradition of assumed racial superiority that Nelson Mandela and many others fought against.

Earliest inhabitants

Located on the southern tip of Africa, the region was first inhabited by groups of nomadic hunters and gatherers. Then, some time before the 17th century, various Bantu-speaking peoples moved into the region, including Sotho, Swazi, Xhosa (Mandela's people) and Zulu. In 1488, a Portuguese explorer named Bartolomeu Diaz became the first European to sail around the tip of South Africa, followed by European settlers. The Dutch, known as Boers (which means farmers), travelled over in the 17th century with the Dutch East India Company. Some stayed, and took land from the native population. They were followed by the British in the 19th century, and resentment quickly grew between the two peoples.

Battle for gold
In 1867, diamonds were discovered in South Africa, followed by gold in 1886. Hoards of foreign prospectors arrived, transforming the country into a landscape of mines and ore dumps. The new arrivals caused conflict with the Boers, and led to Britain's attempt to take control of the Transvaal region in north-east South Africa. Although initially the Boers defeated the British, the Anglo-Boer War of 1899–1902 resulted in the Boers surrendering control of the Transvaal and its mines to Britain.

BANTUS

Some of the earliest inhabitants of South Africa were the nomadic Bantus, or Bushmen. In ancient times, they were the most numerous tribe in the region. Today, only about 26,000 survive, most of who live in the Kalahari Desert.

AFRIKANERS

Afrikaners (formerly called Boers, meaning farmers) are descendents of the original Dutch, German or French settlers. Originally, they spoke Dutch, but as they began to adopt African words into their speech, their language changed, and is now known as Afrikaans.

World War II

During World War II (1939–45), South Africa joined the Allies in fighting against Germany. The war meant that Europe was no longer able to supply South Africa with manufactured goods, so the country had to make and process their own supplies. With many whites fighting overseas, large numbers of black workers moved from mining jobs to the new industries in the cities. Mandela was part of this migration when he moved to Johannesburg in 1941.

Founding of the Union

In 1910, the Union of South Africa was formed, comprising the British colonies of Cape of Good Hope and Natal, and the former Boer republics of the Orange Free State and Transvaal. Despite rebellions on the eve of World War I (1914–18), the Union became stronger, and even expanded when it seized control of Namibia (then German Southwest Africa).

The National Party

In 1914, General BM Herzog founded the National Party to protect and promote Afrikaner interests, which he believed were being engulfed by British influence. Herzog was also adamantly opposed to people from different races mixing, initially proposing a 'two-stream' policy that would allow Afrikaners and English to develop separate cultures and traditions. When he became prime minister, Herzog made sure his plans were implemented, and the Afrikaans language was also officially recognized.

The Boer War was between the Dutch settlers, led by General JBM Herzog (left), and the British. The British combated the Boers' guerrilla warfare by rounding up non-combatants and putting them in concentration camps.

Apartheid

In 1948, the Afrikaaner National Party gained power under Daniel Malan. The party introduced the policy of apartheid — which means 'apartness' in the Afrikaans language. Malan attempted to justify it as a 'separate but equal' development, despite the fact that only the white minority had a say in the nation's affairs. Non-whites did not have the same rights as the 4.5 million whites, which meant that 23 million black people couldn't vote in parliamentary elections and many public places and institutions were restricted for the use of one race only.

Birth of apartheid

Until the 20th century, the British authorities had given the vote to all men over 21 who owned property or had money, including blacks. But after the Boer War, the British began to exclude natives from the franchise, largely to help make peace with the Boers, who were fiercely opposed to political rights for Africans.

Inequalities

Under apartheid, Africans, Europeans and Indians had to live in separate areas called bantustans or homelands, and go to separate schools. Selected jobs were reserved for whites. This was justified by promising that Africans would have full rights in their bantustans. In practice, it meant that Africans had the poorest homes, schools and hospitals. The school curriculum drawn up for black children was also vastly inferior to that for whites. Finally, the Prohibition of Mixed Marriages Act forbade inter-racial marriage.

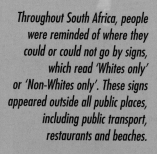

Throughout South Africa, people were reminded of where they could or could not go by signs, which read 'Whites only' or 'Non-Whites only'. These signs appeared outside all public places, including public transport, restaurants and beaches.

STRAND EN SEE
NET BLANKES

BEACH AND SEA
WHITES ONLY →

DANIEL *Malan*

The South African politician, Daniel Malan (1874–1959), believed firmly in white supremacy and a society arranged on a class basis. He became prime minister of South Africa in 1948 and initiated the policy of apartheid and the Group Areas Act, which divided the country into White, Black and Coloured zones.

ORIGIN *of apartheid*

The term apartheid was coined in the 1930s by Afrikaner intellectuals who formed the South African Bureau for Racial Affairs (SABRA). The organization called for a policy of separate development of races. SABRA was founded in opposition to the liberal South African Institute of Race Relations.

Pass laws Every African over 16 had to carry a passbook whenever they left the bantustans. This document showed that the bearer had a job in a white-designated area, and therefore had to travel there. The police had the power to stop Africans and demand to check their passbook. If a person was not carrying one, they could be arrested and imprisoned. Africans who did not have a passbook were condemned to live in areas where job opportunities were small and poverty reigned.

Enforced apartness As a result of the new laws, Africans were ghettoized, living like foreigners in their own country. Ghettos have existed in many countries, but never on such an extreme and massive scale, with racial groups physically separated from each other.

Resistance In 1912, the African National Congress (ANC) was formed. This multiracial nationalist organization aimed to extend the right to vote to the whole population of South Africa and to end racial discrimination there. Yet after 30 years of peaceful petitions to the government, they had achieved no concessions. It would take a new generation of young radicals in the 1940s to plot a more

militant (aggressive) course of action. It was to this new group that Nelson Mandela was drawn on his arrival in Johannesburg.

The old guard The founders of the ANC were Christian-educated members of the African middle-class — mostly doctors, teachers or priests. They wanted the right to vote to be extended from the black middle class to the rest of South Africa. They had no plans to overthrow the white government, instead putting their faith in petitions, pleas and speeches. However, the two South African prime ministers who dominated political life before 1948 — JC Smuts and BM Herzog — were committed segregationists who disregarded all appeals from the ANC to end apartheid.

Under apartheid, blacks lived apart from whites in poor ghettos. Homes and business premises like this barber shop were built using flimsy materials like sacking or old tins. (Image by Jurgen Schadeberg)

Walter Sisulu was one of the founding members of the ANC Youth League, along with Nelson Mandela. (Image by Jurgen Schadeberg)

The Youth League

In 1944, a group of radical young Africans, including Nelson Mandela, Oliver Tambo and Walter Sisulu, formed the ANC Youth League. While acknowledging the important work the ANC had done, they criticized what they saw as its weak leadership. The Youth League aimed to organize mass protests and civil disobedience to force the white government to give rights to Africans.

Defiance Campaign

In 1952, the ANC began a Defiance Campaign against the government's apartheid laws, aiming to make them unworkable. People tore up or burned their passbooks and marched without them into 'whites only' areas. Nelson Mandela, now a member of the National Executive of the ANC, was one of them.

The government began to crack down on the protestors in an increasingly brutal way, and many were arrested, but the protestors had decided to accept imprisonment for their beliefs. The campaign caused the United Nations to pass its first resolution condemning apartheid.

Freedom Charter

In 1954, a non-racial group of 3,000 people from all the anti-apartheid movements within South Africa met at Kliptown near Johannesburg. This Congress of the People produced the Freedom Charter, which set out the movement's objectives for a non-racial, democratic government and equality for all before the law. However, the police broke up the Congress and took the names and addresses of many of those present.

Sharpeville

On March 21st, 1960, one of the other organizations fighting against apartheid, the Pan Africanist Congress (PAC), called for a one-day protest against the pass laws. In Sharpeville, near Johannesburg, a crowd of demonstrators surrounded the police station. Although they were unarmed, the police opened fire on the crowd, killing 69 people and wounding

WALTER *Sisulu*

Walter Sisulu (1912–2003) was a businessman and local leader in Johannesburg when Nelson Mandela met him in 1941. Sisulu had joined the ANC in 1940, and became its general secretary in 1949. He encouraged Mandela to attend meetings of the ANC. The two men became lifelong friends and would later spend many years in prison together.

12

MANDELA *marries*

In 1944, Nelson Mandela married his first wife, Evelyn Mase, with whom he had a son, Thembi. That relationship ended and in 1957, he met Nomzamo Winifred Madikizela who he married in 1958. She was a social worker who also campaigned for the ANC.

many more. Many of them had been shot in the back. The massacre made headlines all around the world. It resulted in the government declaring a State of Emergency and banning the ANC, which meant that its members could be arrested and imprisoned for up to ten years.

The Trials

During the 1950s, Mandela had been banned from public speaking and confined to Johannesburg, arrested and imprisoned. In the latter half of the decade he was one of the accused in the epic Treason Trials. The Treason Trials collapsed in 1961. With the ANC now illegal, the government was using every measure it could to suppress opposition to apartheid. The ANC leaders now had to resume their work from underground headquarters. Mandela now emerged as the leading figure in this new phase of political struggle. He gave an electrifying speech at an All-in African Conference in Pietermaritzburg in March 1961. The conference was held to decide how to react to the government's decision to ban the ANC. Mandela argued that a government which ignored the black majority was 'not valid', and that his people should do anything necessary to fight for their rights.

'How can I be expected to believe that this same racial discrimination, which has been the cause of so much injustice and suffering right through the years, should now operate here to give me a fair and open trial? I consider myself neither morally nor legally obliged to obey laws made by a Parliament in which I am not represented. That the will of the people is the basis of the authority of government, is a principle universally acknowledged as sacred throughout the civilized world.'

Mandela's defence at the Rivonia Trial

Bodies of dead protesters lay on the streets of Sharpeville.

THE *Treason Trials*

The South African government had long tried to imprison the leaders of the ANC and other anti-apartheid organizations. In 1956, the police arrested most of the leaders of the ANC and charged them with treason. The trials lasted for five years, after which every one of the accused was acquitted.

The defendants at the Treason Trials discuss the progress of their case against the government outside the courthouse. (Image by Jurgen Schadeberg)

Armed struggle Mandela and others believed that not only should they continue to fight apartheid but also that they should take up arms against the government. Mandela believed that there were just two choices – 'submit or fight'. In 1961 he formed the military wing of the ANC, called Umkhhonto we Sizwe, meaning 'Spear of the Nation', with the intention of committing acts of sabotage against government buildings, pass offices and electricity pylons. Mandela became its first commander.

The Black Pimpernel

At this time, Mandela went into hiding from the police. He was forced to live apart from his family and to move from place to place to avoid detection by government informers and police spies. But he still managed to appear at important events, often using a disguise as a chauffeur or gardener. Because Mandela was so successful at evading the police, the press began to call him the Black Pimpernel. He travelled to other countries in West and North Africa to motivate support, and also travelled to England, where he met politicians and even had time to do some sightseeing.

Arrest

On August 5th, 1962, Mandela was arrested while disguised as a white friend's chauffeur. He was charged with inciting strikes and with illegally leaving the country. Throughout the trial, Mandela conducted his own defence, and wore traditional African dress to court. However, despite a rigorous defence he was found guilty and sentenced to five years imprisonment. Mandela was sent to prison on Robben Island, a notoriously bleak jail situated on an island some 12 kilometres off the coast of Cape Town.

Rivonia trial

While in prison, Mandela was brought to court again with all the leaders of the ANC who were arrested at Rivonia – their secret headquarters near Johannesburg. They were charged with sabotage and attempting to overthrow the government, offences for which they faced the death sentence. Mandela spoke for over four hours from the witness box, explaining his beliefs in a speech that is now famous. He said that the ideal of a democratic and free society was something which he hoped to live for and to achieve, but, he added, '... if needs be, it is an ideal for which I am prepared to die'. The judge sentenced the defendants to life imprisonment.

Mandela in traditional clothing at his trial in 1962.

BIRTH *of a republic*

In 1961, South Africa became a republic and withdrew from the Commonwealth. The United Nations refused to recognize the republic and South Africa began a 30-year period of international isolation. The country was excluded from international organizations and sporting events and also had economic and trade sanctions imposed.

'All lawful modes of expressing opposition to the principle of white supremacy had been closed by legislation, and we were placed in a position in which we had either to accept a permanent state of inferiority or to defy the government. We chose to defy the government.'

Mandela's defence at the Rivonia Trial

During Mandela's imprisonment, the struggle against apartheid continued. Many countries condemned the sentences, and the United Nations called for the unconditional release of the prisoners. The movement was encouraged by the independence of Zimbabwe, Angola and Mozambique, and by the Black Consciousness movement in South Africa led by Steve Biko. In 1976, the Soweto massacre led to mass strikes and attacks on police stations and government buildings throughout South Africa.

Mandela (left) is pictured here in the prison compound at Robben Island with friend and fellow ANC member Walter Sisulu (right).

Robben Island

Nelson Mandela and the other Rivonia Trial prisoners were incarcerated in South Africa's harshest prison, Robben Island. The island was freezing cold in winter and scorching hot in summer. By day the prisoners crushed rocks, sewed postbags or collected seaweed from the shoreline. They were permitted to only wear short trousers and no shoes, and slept on mats on the floor. Mandela's cell was less than three metres square, lit by a single 40-watt lightbulb. He was confined there for 16 hours every day.

Treatment of prisoners

Prisoners on Robben Island were at first allowed to receive and send one letter every six months. These were heavily censored and often deliberately not posted. Officially, prisoners were allowed two visits a year but Mandela saw his wife just three times in five years. He was not even allowed to attend the funerals of his mother or son when they died. Despite these harsh conditions, he remained determined never to let his spirit be broken.

STEVE *Biko*

Steve Biko (1946–77) was a black activist and founder of the Black Consciousness movement. He studied medicine at Natal University, where he first became involved in politics as a student union leader. He was a popular figure, with his encouragement of black self-reliance, but was frequently detained by police. In 1977, he was arrested and died 26 days later, a result of brain damage sustained during beatings and neglect at the hands of prison staff. He has never been convicted of any crime.

WINNIE *Mandela*

While Mandela was in prison, his wife Winnie did not cease campaigning. She was repeatedly detained without trial and tortured, jailed and even suffered an attempted murder. In 1977, she was put under house arrest in a small village in the right-wing heartland of the Orange Free State. The house had no running water or electricity, and she was confined there at night, weekends and holidays under police guard.

Black Consciousness

In the 1970s, a new generation of young radicals, headed by Steve Biko, took up the cause and became known as the Black Consciousness movement. Biko believed that blacks should not be dependent upon white society but should be aware and proud of their own identity.

Soweto

In 1976, the government announced that half the school curriculum would be taught in Afrikaans, the language of the white minority. Many teachers did not speak this language, and many children did not understand it. A student demonstration was held in Soweto in June. It started peacefully but at one point police panicked and started firing. They killed more than 500 young protesters, many of whom were simply running away. Afterwards, Africans erupted in a fury of anger, attacking police stations and government buildings.

Despite the imprisonment of her husband and the attention of the police, Winnie Mandela remained a high-profile campaigner for the anti-apartheid movement.

The funerals for the victims of the Soweto massacre were highly emotional events.

'Release Mandela'

The government hoped that the prisoners on Robben Island would be forgotten, but the anti-apartheid movement continued to fight for their release. In fact, the movement to free Mandela went global, with the United Nations calling for his release and demonstrations held all around the world. Many countries imposed trade and sporting sanctions, leaving South Africa increasingly isolated. Nelson Mandela had become the most famous political prisoner in the world.

PW Botha was president until 1989 when he retired because of ill health.

Total Strategy In 1978,

PW Botha became prime minister of South Africa and introduced his Total Strategy — a plan of action designed to solve the country's problems. He hoped it would appease both whites and blacks. It relaxed some of the laws restricting blacks, but at the same time gave greater powers to the security forces. Botha aimed to reform the system rather than replace it, so the protests continued.

International sanctions

In order to put additional pressure on the government, the ANC and the unions campaigned for foreign companies to stop investing in South Africa and for countries to boycott South African goods.

A large blow to the government was dealt when, in the mid-1980s, American firms began to close down their offices in the country. The US Congress also encouraged American companies not to invest in South Africa.

The UDF In 1983, the United

Democratic Front was formed. This new non-racial organization was composed of 586 political, trade union, religious, student and women's groups — giving it a membership of more than two million people of all races. It accepted the Freedom Charter and worked with the banned ANC, launching a new widespread campaign called 'Release Mandela!'

PW Botha

The South African political leader Pieter Willem Botha was born in 1916 and became prime minister in 1978. Botha initiated some limited reforms of apartheid policies and began negotiations with Nelson Mandela, but he also harshly repressed dissent.

18

The world is watching

By now, the world was watching nightly news reports of clashes between police and protesters in South Africa. Many hundreds of people were attending funerals of those who had died at the hands of the police or white vigilantes. The townships had become ungovernable. Despite British Prime Minister Margaret Thatcher's support for the Nationalists, the Commonwealth condemned the South African government. Mandela's name began to appear in graffiti, on banners and in songs everywhere. In July 1988, 70,000 people filled Wembley Stadium in London to mark Nelson Mandela's imminent birthday in prison. The concert was televised throughout the globe.

Change will come

During the 1980s, the South African government had offered to release Nelson Mandela many times, on condition that he agreed to be banished to the Transkei bantustan. Each time, he refused. In 1982, he was moved from Robben Island to Pollsmoor Prison on the mainland in Cape Town, where he was allowed to receive visitors. Anxious to prevent more violence in the country, Mandela began at last to talk to the government. These secret meetings would eventually lead to his freedom.

Mandela in prison

Mandela had managed to smuggle out his autobiography while he was on Robben Island. Now he began to experience better conditions and fewer restrictions in prison. He was able to study for a law degree, and also spent much time reading and gardening.

'Only free men can negotiate; prisoners cannot enter into contracts. Your freedom and mine cannot be separated.'

Mandela talks about his frustration at being a prisoner.

The 1980s saw a huge rise in the pressure, from both political and popular sources, on the South African government to free Nelson Mandela. Here, crowds wave banners at Wembley Stadium during a concert supporting the release of the black icon.

RELEASE Mandela!

In 1985, a people's march was organised from Cape Town to the Pollsmoor prison, where Mandela was confined, to give him a message. It read: 'You have not sold the birthright of your people to be free, and we will not rest until you are free.'

FW *de Klerk*

Born in 1936, Frederick Willem de Klerk entered parliament in 1972, and was active in the conservative wing of the National Party. When he replaced PW Botha as president, de Klerk projected himself as a conservative who sought only gradual reform of the apartheid system and improved diplomatic relations. No one could have guessed that he would be the president to bring apartheid to an end.

FW de Klerk found it difficult to persuade the black population of South Africa to trust him.

> 'Law and order must be restored ... the full power of the State has to be employed to this end.'
>
> *Louis La Grange, Minister of Law and Order, justifying the State of Emergency declared in South Africa in 1985.*

In 1988, Mandela became ill with tuberculosis. After a spell in hospital, he was moved to a prison governor's house within Victor Verster prison in Paarl, 50 kilometres outside Cape Town, and was allowed greater contact with friends and family.

New president

In 1985, when he was offered freedom on condition that he stop campaigning for the ANC, Mandela responded: 'I cherish my own freedom, but... I will not give any undertaking when you and I, the people, are not free.' In 1989, President Botha resigned due to ill health and FW de Klerk was elected in his place. At first, de Klerk was no supporter of change, but eventually he realised that the country's problems would only get worse, so he began to lead the country in a new direction.

Historic speech

On February 2nd, 1990, in his opening speech to parliament, de Klerk did what no other South African head-of-state had ever done – he announced plans to begin dismantling apartheid, starting with the legalising

of the ANC and other organizations. He promised that he would release hundreds of political prisoners and suspend capital punishment. De Klerk also opened many public places – including beaches, parks, restaurants, buses and libraries – to people of all colours.

Secret talks

Behind the scenes, Nelson Mandela was talking to a secret negotiating committee of the government about his release. In effect, Mandela was dictating his own terms. He demanded the release of his former Robben Island comrades, including Walter Sisulu. They were finally released in October 1989. Mandela met de Klerk for the first time in December 1989 at Tuynhuys, the official presidential office. Mandela stressed that the apartheid state should not just be softened but totally abandoned. De Klerk listened but left in disagreement with Mandela.

Surprise release

Then, on February 10th, 1990, de Klerk called Mandela to Tuynhuys again. He told Mandela that he would be released the next day! This came as a complete surprise

REASONS *for change*

There were many reasons for the government's change in attitude. South Africa was increasingly isolated from the rest of the world, and sanctions were hurting its economy. Even the country's few friends were losing patience. The ongoing State of Emergency had resulted in thousands of people in detention, yet there was still no law and order in the townships. At the time, South Africa was fighting an undeclared war in neighbouring Angola, which was proving very expensive. Now even the army was calling for change.

This picture shows a group of African women who were injured in the war between South Africa and Angola.

to Mandela, and at first he refused. He wanted a week's notice to allow his family and the ANC time to prepare. But de Klerk had already informed the press, so he did not want to change the date. De Klerk planned to fly Mandela to Johannesburg and officially release him there, but Mandela objected. Mandela wanted to walk out of the gates of the prison and greet the people of Cape Town. De Klerk consented – but only if Mandela agreed to be released the next day. They sealed the deal with a glass of whiskey, which the teetotal Mandela only pretended to drink.

Prison guards look out from the cottage where Nelson Mandela was being held prisoner. Photographers would regularly try to get pictures of the famous prisoner.

Nelson Mandela's release was set for 3.00 pm, but his day began at dawn. The extreme suddenness of the release meant that the arrangements had to be made in a hurry. In all the many details, Mandela hardly had time to dwell on the momentousness of the occasion.

FAMILY & FRIENDS `00:30`

Nelson Mandela's first minutes of the day were spent telephoning his wife Winnie, his friend Walter Sisulu, and colleagues in Cape Town to tell them of his release later that day. They all arranged to fly in on a chartered plane to be there for the historic occasion. Then he drafted a speech to deliver to his supporters, and eventually went to bed in the early hours of the morning.

The ANC were kept informed hour by hour about Mandela's release.

LAST MOMENTS `04:30`

On a cloudless summer's day in Cape Town, Nelson Mandela woke, exercised, washed, ate breakfast, and continued work on his speech. The prison doctor gave him a brief check-up, after which he telephoned colleagues at the ANC and the UDF, to request that they come to the prison to help him prepare for his release. Mandela also planned to say goodbye personally to all the prison officers.

Nelson Mandela anticipates his freedom.

VIEWS *from the ground*

'I stood for hours on the parade in Cape Town hoping to catch a glimpse of Nelson Mandela after his historic release. Blacks and whites mingled in close proximity in a light-hearted, jovial atmosphere. The Parade was the most crowded I had ever seen it in 15 years. Usually it was packed with cars... but on this day it was wall-to-wall people of every race you could imagine.'

Andrew Malcolm, a bystander

'I was at home in Cape Town. I had been waiting for this day all of my life... now one year after graduation I found myself all alone at home watching the TV screen, trying to get a sense of history in the making. Then... there he was – Nelson the hero, the David in our battle of apartheid... a moment I thought I would never witness.'

Noel Southgate, then a graduate in South Africa

Officials at Victor Verster prison had to deal with overwhelming press interest in Mandela's forthcoming release.

PLANS ARE MADE `07:00`

Early in the morning, members of the Reception Committee, who were to oversee Mandela's release, arrived at the cottage. They discussed the arrangements for Mandela's appearance at the Grand Parade in Cape Town. Soon, the cottage was filled with people. Amidst the busy preparations, Mandela had to find time to pack his belongings in the boxes and crates the prison service had supplied to him. In his years in prison on the mainland, he had accumulated enough to fill over a dozen containers.

DESMOND TUTU `12:30`

It had not yet been decided where Mandela would spend his first night of freedom. He wanted to stay in the black townships of Cape Town, to show his solidarity with the people. But his colleagues advised him to stay with Archbishop Desmond Tutu.

Mandela was advised to go to the home of Archbishop Desmond Tutu by officials.

THE CRITICAL MOMENT February 11th, 1990

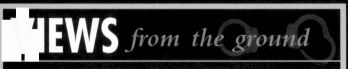

WINNIE'S ARRIVAL   14:00

Winnie, Walter and the others arrived, giving the cottage a mood of celebration. They all sat down to a last meal, prepared by Warrant Officer Swart (right), with whom Mandela had formed a close companionship over the years. After the meal, Mandela embraced Swart, and the other officers at the cottage, and began to say his farewells.

Warrant Officer Swart saying goodbye to Nelson Mandela.

NEWS *from the ground*

The release was *'another significant step on the road to the non-racial, democratic South Africa.'*

US President Bush (Sr)

LEAVING THE COTTAGE ⟨15:55⟩

At 3.00 pm, a presenter from South African TV phoned Mandela to request that he get out of the car just before the gate so they could film him walking to freedom. He agreed, but became increasingly anxious at being behind schedule. Just before 4.00 pm, the cavalcade was finally ready to take Mandela to Cape Town. The cars set off from the cottage, stopping short of the gate so Nelson and Winnie could walk the rest of the way. Just by the gate, Mandela saw for the first time the huge crowd of reporters and supporters. He had only expected a small group of wardens and their families!

Mandela's cavalcade set off for Cape Town, stopping just short of the gate to allow Mandela to meet the crowds.

CHEERS FOR MANDELA ⟨16:00⟩

When Mandela was next to the gate, hundreds of cameras started clicking and reporters shouted questions, while the crowd cheered wildly. He took Winnie's hand for the last yards, finding the commotion disorientating. When a reporter thrust a long furry microphone towards him, he recoiled, thinking it was some new kind of weapon. When he raised his right fist in the ANC power salute, the crowd roared. Then, just minutes later, Mandela climbed into another car for the drive to Cape Town.

Nelson and Winnie Mandela were greeted by jubilent crowds when they walked from the prison gates.

ON TO CAPETOWN

The drive took the newly free 71-year-old Mandela through the prosperous white farmlands. Even here, people lined the road to catch a glimpse of the motorcade. Some white people even raised their fists in the ANC salute, and Mandela was so moved he stopped and got out of the car to thank one family. While Mandela was driven to Cape Town, 60,000 people were waiting with huge banners at the Grand Parade, a great open square in front of the old City Hall. Many had been there since early in the morning, and were becoming increasingly restless. Some had fainted in the heat or were injured by crowd surges. At one point, a water main burst and people scrambled to it for handfuls of cool water.

Mandela sets off to Cape Town.

Crowds had gathered all day to greet Mandela in South Africa's capital.

VIEWS *from the ground*

'The time for talking has come.'
President Kaunda of Zambia

'A triumph for national resistance and international pressure over apartheid's custodians at home and its apologists abroad.'
Sonny Ramphal (Commonwealth Secretary-General)

'Do you see how lovely the people of South Africa can be?'
Young man at the City Hall

'We are one nation, black and white. We are one people.'
Old man at City Hall

OUT OF CONTROL? `16:30`

Meanwhile, in the backstreets around the Grand Parade, police opened fire at groups of youths, who they claimed were smashing windows and looting shops. The police also fired birdshot and rubber bullets to disperse sections of the crowd. Mobile medical units treated the injured, including children, who were lying on stretchers. In other parts of the country, crowds celebrating Mandela's release were also attacked by police.

Several riots took place during the day of Mandela's release.

GRAND PARADE `17:00`

By the time they reached the outskirts of Cape Town, the immensity of the welcoming rally was becoming apparent, as hordes of people streamed towards the Grand Parade. Mandela's driver at first tried to take his important passenger through the crowd, but turned back when a huge crowd surrounded the car, knocking on the windows, jumping on the top and rocking it. The driver was panicking, so Mandela suggested they cool down at the house of his friend and attorney, Dullah Omar. After refreshing drinks, they drove to the back entrance of the Grand Parade.

WAITING 17:15

The crowd were urged to be patient by Reverend Allan Boesak.

It was dusk when Nelson Mandela eventually addressed the crowds at the Grand Parade. Two anti-apartheid clerics, the Reverend Frank Chicane and the Reverend Allan Boesak, had urged patience as the hours passed. Although many of the original 60,000 dispersed, some 10,000 remained. Similar crowds gathered at towns and cities throughout the country. The centres of Johannesburg and Soweto, normally quiet on a Sunday, were busy with jubilant people. Mandela's speech was broadcast live around the world – although South African viewers had to wait for several minutes before it was shown.

Mandela's supporters eagerly awaited his famous speech.

MANDELA IS READY 17:45

Mandela was led through the back entrance and up to the top floor. When he walked out onto the balcony, the crowd cheered and clapped, raising flags and banners above their heads. The cheering and chanting grew louder as Mandela raised his fist into the air. He took out the speech he had written only hours earlier, but when he reached into his pocket for his glasses, Mandela realised he had left them in prison. He had to borrow Winnie's glasses to read the speech!

Nelson Mandela delivered his speech to a crowd of more than 10,000 people.

THE SPEECH STARTS

In his speech, Mandela thanked all the people across the globe that had campaigned for his release, reserving special thanks for all the anti-apartheid organizations in South Africa itself. He also acknowledged his family, whose pain and suffering, he believed, 'was far greater than my own'. He was careful to tell people that he had not done any deals with the government for his release. Then he praised de Klerk, but warned people that the fight against apartheid was not yet over. 'The sight of freedom looming on the horizon should encourage us to redouble our efforts,' he said.

PHONECALLS FROM OLD FRIENDS

`19:15`

When the speech was over, Mandela was hustled back into a car and driven away. Even now, black faces lined the streets, singing and calling his name. That evening he stayed at the house of Archbishop Desmond Tutu, where he was met by his family and friends. During the evening, he had a phonecall that was very important to him: his old friend Oliver Tambo spoke to him from Stockholm, where he was recovering from a stroke.

Mandela spent his first night of freedom in the home of Desmond Tutu.

VIEWS *from the ground*

'I stand here before you not as a prophet, but as a humble servant of you, the people.'

'I have fought against white domination and I have fought against black domination. I have cherished the ideal of a democratic and free society in which all peoples live together in harmony and with equal opportunity. It is an ideal which I hope to live for and to achieve, but if needs be, it is an ideal for which I am prepared to die.'

Quotes from Mandela's speech

*T*he day after his release, the real work for Nelson Mandela and the ANC began. Apartheid was still in place and so was the government that had upheld it for so long at such great cost to millions of South African lives. Mandela embarked on a punishing schedule of meetings, working hard to negotiate a new constitution and helping the ANC to become a proper political party.

Foreign travels

In June 1990, Mandela went on a six-week tour of Europe and North America to meet with world leaders. In Paris he met President Mitterand, and travelled through Switzerland, Italy, The Netherlands and England. On his arrival in New York, he was greeted by a ticker-tape parade through the streets, which were crowded with more than a million people – each eager to catch a glimpse. Mandela met President Bush (Sr), urging him not to halt sanctions until apartheid was completely destroyed and an interim government was in place. Before his return to South Africa, he also made trips to the African countries of Uganda, Kenya and Mozambique.

Limited progress

Shortly after Mandela's release, the government signed an agreement with the ANC to repeal repressive laws, release political prisoners and continue negotiating. Yet the violence in the country continued, with more than 3,000 people killed in 1990 alone. Mandela was keen to speed up the process of dismantling

Mandela inspects the troops during his visit to Britain.

INKATHA

Inkatha is a political organization formed in 1975 by Chief Gatsha Buthelezi (right). It is named after the strong headgear worn by Zulu women to carry heavy loads. Buthelezi is the leader of six million Zulus, the biggest ethnic group in South Africa. Although its aims were to create a non-racial democratic system in South Africa, Inkatha had tried to work with the white government, which led to criticism from the ANC.

apartheid and rebuilding the country. He persuaded the ANC to suspend the armed struggle, in order to show good faith. A month later the government lifted the State of Emergency. However, it became clear to many that de Klerk still had race-founded prejudices.

Inkatha One serious problem was the violence in Natal, where Chief Buthelezi's conservative Inkatha movement had declared war on the ANC and were burning entire villages down, killing many people. Mandela and others began to suspect that the conflict was being fuelled by the South African police, backed by the government, to discredit and weaken African movements. Mandela visited Inkatha leaders, telling them: 'take your guns, your knives and your pangas, and throw them into the sea!'

ANC conference

In July 1991, the ANC held their annual conference in Johannesburg, the first to be held inside South Africa for 30 years. More than 2,200 delegates attended the conference. Mandela was elected president without opposition, and talk turned to transforming an illegal underground liberation movement into a legal mass political party. As Mandela said in his speech, 'The struggle is not over.'

Nelson Mandela and FW de Klerk show off the Nobel Peace Prizes which they were awarded.

Negotiations

At the end of 1991, the Convention for a Democratic South Africa (CODESA) was held in Johannesburg. Representatives from 18 organizations met to negotiate a new constitution, but each party had a different agenda and the talks failed. A whites-only referendum in May 1992 showed two-thirds in favour of negotiations, prompting a new round of talks, CODESA II. This also failed to bring a breakthrough. It was not until the next year that the ANC and the government agreed what do. They decided that a five-year government of national unity, made up of representatives from all the political parties, would write the new constitution for the country. A date was set for the election: April 27th, 1994.

Tragedies

During the lead-up to the election, the new South Africa experienced a wave of violence. In June 1992, Inkatha supporters shot or hacked to death 49 men, women and children in a black settlement called Boipatong. Witnesses claim they saw police trucks carrying in Inkatha people. The ANC broke off talks with the government in protest until de Klerk called a halt to the violence. Then, just months later, the popular black activist Chris Hani was shot dead in front of his house by a member of an extreme right-wing white supremacist group. The assassination led to mass rioting. Mandela begged the people to be calm and not to stop the progress towards majority rule by peaceful means.

The election

Despite the violence, the plans for elections were not disrupted. A lot of work had to be done to educate black voters, who would be voting for the first time in their lives (and many of whom were illiterate). People's forums went all over

NOBEL *prize*

In 1993, Mandela and FW de Klerk were both awarded the Nobel Peace Prize and travelled to Oslo, Norway to receive it. 'Five years ago, people would have seriously questioned the sanity of anyone who predicted that Mr. Mandela and I would be joint recipients of the 1993 Nobel Peace Prize,' de Klerk said in his Nobel lecture. 'And yet both of us are here before you today.'

DIVORCE *from Winnie*

Since leaving prison, Mandela had had little time to spend with his family, and in 1992 his marriage to Winnie broke up. Winnie had been convicted on a kidnapping charge stemming from the abduction of a 14-year-old boy who was later found beaten to death. Mandela had stood by her during the trial, but eventually acknowledged that the marriage was over.

Nelson Mandela divorced his second wife Winnie in 1992.

the country to speak to men and women and answer their questions. On the day of the election, 23 million people lined up patiently at polling stations to cast their votes. The mood in the country became more positive and the violence ceased.

The ANC won the election with 62.6% of the vote and Mandela became South Africa's first black president.

Millions of black voters queued patiently for hours to vote for the first time.

NEW *home*

After his release, Mandela had a house built in Qunu, in the Transkei, where he was born. In the grounds, he has built an exact replica of the warden's bungalow in which he was held at Victor Verster jail. Every year, he holds a Christmas party here, attended by thousands of children and parents.

President Mandela After the election, world leaders came to South Africa to pay tribute to Mandela. However, after the celebrations, Mandela faced innumerable tasks. The new ANC-led government inherited a country in economic decline, with widespread corruption and racial division. He was committed to eradicating the extensive and damaging repercussions of the apartheid system, and in particular the inequality between blacks and whites. But he also had to maintain a growing economy that could provide jobs for everyone. Change was slow – many Africans were still very poor, and there were violent protests in many parts of the country.

New government Mandela's government included African, Indian and white ministers, and even some former supporters of apartheid. In the main, these ministers were inexperienced, and Mandela frequently took matters into his own hands as the quickest means to an end, despite the ANC's long history of collective decision-making. He allocated 4.2 billion rand to reform health,

housing, and education systems, and to promote economic growth. He promised, among other things, to build 300,000 new homes a year by the turn of the century. Mandela also passed the Restitution of Land Rights Act, which returned lands taken from blacks under apartheid.

New constitution The process of writing up the new constitution took almost two years, and produced one of the most ambitious constitutions in the world. On the day in 1996 when it was passed,

Nelson Mandela meeting Bill Clinton, who became a close personal friend of the new South African president.

delegates and spectators in the parliament chamber broke out spontaneously into jubilant celebrations. 'This is the day when South Africa is truly born,' said Cyril Ramaphosa, chairman of the assembly. It outlawed discrimination on the basis of race, gender, sexual orientation, age, pregnancy or marital status. It also granted its citizens rights to adequate housing, food, water, health care, education and social security – all of which were withheld from the black majority during the apartheid era.

Truth and Reconciliation Commission

In 1996, the Truth and Reconciliation Commission was set up to investigate the political crimes of the apartheid era. The Commission spent two-and-a-half years compiling the report. Chaired by Archbishop Desmond Tutu, it took more than 20,000 statements from individual victims of human rights abuses. The aim was not to punish the perpetrators, but to ask them to apologize in public. Mandela said, 'If we don't forgive them, then that feeling of bitterness and revenge will always be there.'

Commission findings

Many people were called before the Commission, including FW de Klerk, who begged forgiveness for the apartheid years, and Winnie Mandela, who was implicated in the violent behaviour of her bodyguards. The Commission condemned the human rights abuses of the apartheid state, accusing President Botha of involvement in many of the atrocities, despite the fact that he refused to attend the hearings. In 1998, the Commission published its report, in spite of a last-minute attempt by de Klerk to have his name removed in connection to apartheid-era injustices. Many black people in South Africa felt that the Commission let a great number of guilty people off too easily. They also believed that apologies alone were not enough.

Sports supporter

Mandela chose a powerful means to bridge the racial divide – sport. As president, he made public appearances at important rugby matches – traditionally a game played only by white South Africans. He was present at the final of the Rugby World Cup in 1995 and, when South Africa beat

Mandela regularly appeared in front of huge sporting crowds wearing the traditional colours of South Africa's teams.

New Zealand, he was seen presenting the trophy to the South African captain Francois Pienaar, dressed in the green springbock jersey. Mandela was also fundamental in luring the Cricket World Cup to South Africa in 2003 and even appeared in television adverts promoting the event.

35

> 'I dream of the realization of the unity of Africa, whereby its leaders combine in their efforts to solve the problems of this continent. I dream of our vast deserts, of our forests, of all our great wildernesses.'
>
> *Mandela talks about African unity*

One of his many public appearances after retirement from political life included this one with the Spice Girls.

As president, Nelson Mandela became a great ambassador for his country and a symbol of freedom and humanity everywhere. Every year, he received about 5,000 requests for appearances and official engagements, of which he could only accept a small proportion. Even so, his diary was booked for months ahead, with every hour of every day accounted for. Archbishop Desmond Tutu said of him, 'He leaves me panting in exhaustion just looking at the schedule he keeps.'

Diplomat
Mandela's great talents for compassion, humour and political shrewdness allowed him to maintain relations with leaders from all ends of the political spectrum, from American presidents to the Cuban leader Fidel Castro. He also kept diplomatic ties with Colonel Gaddafi and Arafat, men seen as dangerous extremists by America. Mandela remembered that these men helped the ANC during their long fight against apartheid.

Remarriage
In his 70s, Mandela met and became close friends with Grace Machel, the widow of the former leader of Mozambique. She, like Mandela, has long been a campaigner for human rights, in particular for women and children.

In 1998, on his 80th birthday, Mandela married Grace, saying of her, 'She is my life'. Between them, they have 45 children and grandchildren, with whom Nelson spends as much time as possible.

Charity work
In 1995, Mandela founded The Nelson Mandela Children's Fund with a personal contribution of 30% of his salary. Since then, the charity has raised more than £20 million and distributed approximately £6 million into its projects to alleviate child poverty. In recent years, the Children's Fund has focused its attention on children and families affected by the spread of HIV and AIDS.

AIDS epidemic In South Africa, four million people are HIV-positive. On average, 600 people a day die from AIDS-related illnesses and more than 660,000 children have lost both their parents to HIV and AIDS. Part of the problem has been the reluctance of South African leaders to talk about an issue that many Africans feel is 'private'. When he was president, Mandela feared upsetting voters by talking about the disease. The current president, Thabo Mbeki has also proved reluctant to speak on the issue and has even expressed doubts about the extent to which the AIDS virus has spread in South Africa. Since his retirement, however, Mandela has campaigned relentlessly on the issue and raised much-needed funds.

AID *for AIDS*

In 1991, a breakthrough in the fight against AIDS was achieved when a group of 39 multinational pharmaceutical companies dropped their battle to stop South Africa importing cheaper, generic AIDS drugs.

AIDS campaigners in South Africa try to raise awareness about the disease. This, combined with greater access to new drugs to combat the virus, means there should be more hope for South Africa in the future.

Mandela pictured with his wife, Grace Machel, whom he married on his 80th birthday.

Despite retiring from politics, Mandela maintains a hectic schedule, travelling extensively to fulfil his duties. Here he is talking to the head of the UN, Kofi Annin.

Thabo Mbeki, Nelson Mandela's successor was hand picked by Mandela to be his Deputy President. In 1999, Mbeki became the new President of South Africa.

Retirement

In 1999, after five years as president, Mandela retired and returned to his home in the Transkei where he had been born. Yet he still travels and meets world leaders and is one of the world's most famous and inspirational men, celebrated everywhere. His views on world events – from strife in his own country to the war in Iraq – continues to command attention. Today, Nelson Mandela jokes about when he will retire from his retirement!

Successor

Mandela's deputy, Thabo Mbeki, succeeded him as president. A long-term anti-apartheid activist, Mbeki spent many years in exile in Britain and Russia, where he trained as a guerrilla fighter. Acutely aware of the difficulty of filling Mandela's shoes as president, he has focused on raising living standards for the black population and making sure the economy is in a good state.

Health scare

Despite the fact that Nelson Mandela is in his eighties and can appear fragile, he is remarkably fit and generally healthy. He travels everywhere with his own doctor. In July 2001, however, Mandela was diagnosed as having prostate cancer, and underwent seven months of radiotherapy in Cape Town. 'I am going to stay on top of this little development,' he said, with typical humour and understatement. In February 2002, he announced that the treatment had been successful.

Art for charity

In 2002, Mandela turned his hand to another skill – painting. He produced a series of colourful charcoal and pastel drawings inspired by his time on Robben Island, and they were sold to raise money for his children's charity. The drawings went on display in

WINNIE'S *future*

In 2003, Winnie Mandela was in court again, this time on charges of fraud and theft. She was sentenced to five years in prison. Like a modern-day Robin Hood, she was convicted of fraudulently acquiring loans for people who were desperately poor. Winnie continues to be a controversial figure, but one who commands great support among the people of South Africa.

'If any man on earth has earned the right to speak his mind, then Mandela has.'

Bill Clinton

London, and on Robben Island – which is now South Africa's first World Heritage Site. Part of it is now named after its most famous prisoner, Nelson Mandela.

Mandela movie In 2003, a film based on the life of Nelson Mandela was announced, starring US actor Morgan Freeman, famous for his part in the movie *The Shawshank Redemption* (1994). To prepare for the role, Freeman arranged with Mandela to meet up whenever they were within 1,000 miles of each other. Mandela's autobiography, *Long Walk To Freedom*, is the basis for the film. In an interview Freeman said, 'I am honoured and terrified that I won't live up to the job of really presenting this man'. The British director, Shekhar Kapur said, 'Mandela is a spiritual leader like Gandhi. He does not need to fight a bloody battle in order to win'.

'Give us, the people, the chance freely to determine the future of our country!'

Thabo Mbeki speaking upon his election as the new President of South Africa.

The actor Morgan Freeman has played many roles throughout his film career, but in the upcoming film of Mandela's life, he will act perhaps the most important part of his film career, that of Nelson Mandela.

South Africa faces many tough challenges in the future. Even with apartheid dismantled, the bulk of the economy, including the land, remains mainly white-owned, with many of the best jobs going to whites. Poverty and inequality continue to be major issues, and murder rates are ten times higher than in the United States.

A band playing during the spectacular opening ceremony for the African Union. (Image by Jurgen Schadeberg)

Ongoing battle The most serious problem in South Africa is the spread of AIDS. One in nine people are infected with HIV and more than 150 children are born HIV-positive in the country every day. In 2002, the Nelson Mandela Children's Fund joined forces with the Diana, Princess of Wales Memorial Fund (set up after her death in 1997) to launch a massive initiative in support of children and families affected by the crisis. Mandela and Diana had planned a joint offensive in 1997 when she visited South Africa, just five months before she died. After her death, Mandela praised Diana's commitment to humanitarian causes, saying, 'Her inspiration must continue to change lives now and in the future.'

NGO *networks*

Non-governmental Organizations (NGOs) have created a vast network of organizations in South Africa to help combat the spread of AIDS. The National Association for People With Aids (NAPWA) has become a more powerful voice for those living with the virus. In February 2000, the government launched the National AIDS Council (NAC) made up of representatives from the government, business, NGOs and the medical sector.

A young family struck down by the AIDS virus.

Powerful party

Some people fear that the ANC is becoming too powerful. Its aim to achieve a two-thirds majority in a national election would allow it to make sweeping changes without consulting any of the other political parties. It also wants to change the clause in the constitution so that a president can serve more than the maximum two terms that are allowed by the present constitution.

Some people worry that the other parties in South African politics are already too weak to provide an effective opposition and this would damage democracy.

Brain drain

South Africa also faces the challenge of finding ways to encourage its skilled professional workers to stay in the country, as many thousands choose to emigrate abroad every year in search of a better life. Many leave because of the high levels of crime, rising unemployment and fear of the AIDS epidemic. The government is trying to reverse this trend, giving financial and business support to those companies who are training black workers to fill the gaps left by emigrating professionals. Other people, however, believe that the government should find ways to encourage emigration to South Africa from other countries.

The African Union

In 2002, the African Union (AU) was established. At its inauguration, it was made up of 53 African states from all over the continent with the South African president Thabo Mbeki as its first chairman. Basing itself loosely on its northern counterpart, the European Union (EU), the AU's aims are to encourage the spread of democracy throughout the whole of Africa.

'That was one of the things that worried me — to be raised to the position of a semi-god — because then you are no longer a human being. I wanted to be known as Mandela, a man with weaknesses, some of which are fundamental, and a man who is committed, but never the less, sometimes he fails to live up to expectations.'

Nelson Mandela

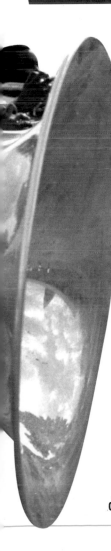

TIMELINE

1400–1799

• 1488: Portuguese explorer Bartolomeu Diaz becomes the first European to sail round the tip of South Africa.

• 1600s: Bantu-speaking peoples move into the region that is modern-day South Africa, including the Sotho, Swazi, Zulu and Xhosa (Mandela's people).

• 1652: Dutch settlers found Cape Town on the very tip of southern Africa to act as a port-of-call for traders travelling on the way from Europe to the Far East.

• 1795: The British invade Cape Town and temporarily seize the colony from the Dutch.

1800–1899

• 1806: The British attempt to occupy Cape Town for the second time.

• 1814: The British purchase Cape Town and the surrounding area for £6 million.

• 1836–56: The Dutch – who wish to escape British rule – found the republics of Transvaal, the Orange Free State and Cape Colony.

• 1867: Large reserves of diamonds are discovered at Kimberley, Cape Colony.

• 1886: Gold is discovered in Transvaal. This, together with the earlier diamond find, encourages a rush of European prospectors, who come into conflict with the Boers (Dutch farmers).

• 1899–1902: Anglo-Boer War results in the Boers surrendering control of the Transvaal and its diamond and gold mines to Britain.

1900–1919

• 1910: The Union of South Africa is formed, comprising the Cape of Good Hope, Natal, Orange Free State and Transvaal.

• 1910: Pass laws require black people to carry travel, work, residential and curfew passes. People could be punished for not producing them when requested.

• 1911: New laws bar blacks from working in many types of occupation.

• 1912: The first national association for black people, the South African Native National Congress (SANNC), is founded.

• 1913: The Native Land Act makes it illegal for blacks to own land except in a few native reserves that make up just over seven per cent of the total land.

• 1914: General BM Herzog founds the National Party to promote Afrikaner interests.

• 1914–18: World War I is fought.

• July 18, 1918: Nelson Mandela is born.

1920–1952

• 1923: The Urban Areas Act is passed by the South African government and creates certain areas, usually located on the outskirts of cities, where blacks could be forced to live.

• 1923: The South African Native National Congress (SANNC), which was founded in 1912, changes its name to the African National Congress (ANC).

• 1924: Certain unskilled jobs become available to white applicants only.

• 1933: The United Party, formed when the Nationalist Party joined forces with the opposition South African Party, comes to power in the South African government.

• 1944: Nelson Mandela, Oliver Tambo, Walter Sisulu and several others form the ANC Youth League, which has a more radical agenda than the ANC.

• 1944: Nelson Mandela marries his first wife, Evelyn Mase. (They divorce in 1958.)

• March 1950: Mandela joins the ANC National Executive.

• 1952: the Defiance Campaign is started, which aimed to use massive civil disobedience to render apartheid unworkable.

1400–1799   ## 1800–1899   ## 1900–1919   ## 1920–1952

1952–1959

• 1952: Mandela is elected president of the ANC Youth League and deputy president of the ANC itself.

• Mandela opens a law practice in Johannesburg with his friend Oliver Tambo as partner.

• 1954–5: The Congress of the People, composed of anti-apartheid organizations throughout South Africa, draws up the Freedom Charter calling for equality for all. Nelson Mandela is one of the organizers.

• 1956: Mandela and other black activists are arrested and tried for high treason. These Treason Trials last until 1961, when all the accused are acquitted.

• 1958: Mandela marries Nomzamo Winifred Madikizela, who becomes popularly known as Winnie Mandela.

1960–1969

• March 1960: The Sharpeville Massacre occurs in which 69 blacks protesting the Pass laws are killed by police, with many more injured, making headlines worldwide. The trouble resulting from this incident leads to the banning of the ANC by the government.

• 1961: Mandela becomes Commander-in-Chief of Umkhonto we Sizwe ('Spear of the Nation'), the military wing of the ANC.

• August 1962: Mandela is arrested and later sentenced to six years' imprisonment on Robben Island, off the coast of Cape Town.

• October 1963: Mandela is charged with sabotage at the famous Rivonia trial.

• June 1964: Mandela is sentenced to life imprisonment on Robben Island.

1970–1989

• 1976: The Soweto Massacre sees more than 500 students protesting against apartheid killed by police.

• 1977: The black activist Steve Biko is arrested and dies 26 days later in prison.

• 1982: Mandela is moved from Robben Island to Pollsmoor Prison on the mainland.

• 1985: Mandela is offered freedom on condition that he renounces political violence. He turns this offer down.

• 1987: Mandela begins secret talks with the government.

• 1988: Mandela moves into a private bungalow in the grounds of Victor Verster prison near Cape Town.

• October 1989: Mandela's former Robben Island comrades, including Walter Sisulu, are released.

• December 1989: Mandela meets President FW de Klerk. This meeting is followed by others, after which de Klerk eventually agrees to Mandela's unconditional release.

1990–1999

• 2 February 1990: the South African government announces the unbanning of the ANC and the release of many political prisoners.

• 11 February, 1990: Nelson Mandela is released from prison after 10,000 days.

• July 1990: Mandela is elected president of the ANC.

• 1993: Nelson Mandela and FW de Klerk are awarded the Nobel Peace Prize.

• 10 May, 1994: Mandela becomes president of South Africa in the country's first elections in which everyone can vote.

• 1996: The Truth and Reconciliation Commission is set up to investigate the political crimes of the apartheid era.

• 1998: Mandela divorces Winnie Mandela and marries Grace Machel.

• June 1999: Mandela retires from public life at the end of his five-year term as president.

1952–1959
1960–1969
1970–1989
1990–1999

GLOSSARY

activist Someone who devotes time and energy to a political or social cause.

Afrikaans An official language of the Republic of South Africa, closely related to Dutch and Flemish.

Afrikaner An inhabitant of the Republic of South Africa who speaks Afrikaans and is descended from the original Dutch settlers. At first, Afrikaners were farmers, but now they mostly live and work in cities.

ambassador A representative of a country. Countries usually have formal ambassadors who live in embassies in other countries around the world. However, a person may become an informal ambassador, representing their country through their reputation and deeds.

apartheid In South Africa, apartheid was the enforced separation of African, European and Indian people.

Bantu A group of similar languages spoken widely in southern, eastern and central Africa, including Zulu, Swahili and Xhosa; also the name of people who speak any of these languages. The word 'Bantu' means 'people' in Zulu.

bantustans Areas in South Africa where non-whites were forced by the authorities to live under apartheid.

Boer Name given to people in South Africa who are descendants of the original Dutch settlers. These people are now referred to as Afrikaners.

boycott To protest against a person, organization or country by refusing to deal with it or buy products from it.

civil disobedience Legal actions such as marches and demonstrations that protest against unfair laws.

colony A country or region that is being ruled by another country. Between the 16th and 19th centuries, several European nations, including Britain, Spain and France established colonies all around the globe.

coloured Term used in South Africa to describe people of a mixed white and black background.

communist A supporter of a political system in which property and industry are controlled by the government rather than individuals.

conservative An individual or organization that favours the preservation of established customs or values, and opposes change.

constitution A written document that states the aims of a country or organization and sets out how it will be run.

democratic Description of a form of political system in a country in which everyone has equal rights.

detention The confinement of a person awaiting trial.

dissent In political terms, the expression of disagreement with a prevailing view or political system.

exile A prolonged, usually enforced, absence from your own country.

ghetto A densely populated slum part of a city where the poorest people live. It can also be used to describe a poor region of a town where people from the same ethnic background are forced to live. For example, many black people were forced to live in ghettos in South Africa at the height of the apartheid era.

guerrilla Term used to describe small-scale, often politically motivated warfare, usually to combat a larger force such as the army or police. Rather than confronting a much larger enemy out in the open, guerrillas will use other methods, such as attacking and destroying infrastructure, such as power supplies and transport links.

house arrest Forced confinement, usually in your own house. Many political activists have been kept under house arrest in countries around the world to stop them from creating unrest.

human rights The rights of individuals to freedom and justice.

Inkatha A Zulu political organisation formed in 1975 by Chief Gatsha Buthelezi, which aimed to create a non-racial democratic system in South Africa but which tried to work with the white government. Following Nelson Mandela's release, supporters of Inkatha and the ANC were involved in a series of violent clashes which many felt were stirred up by the white government.

legislation Refers to the process of making a law, or to the law itself.

migration The movement of people from one place, region, or country to another.

negotiations Peaceful discussions to solve a dispute.

nomad A person who moves from place to place to find food and land for animals to graze.

petition A letter signed by many people requesting that a government or organization do or change something.

radical Someone who favours extreme or fundamental changes to a political, economic or social system.

reconciliation The coming together of opposing groups to settle their differences.

sabotage The deliberate damage or destruction of equipment or machinery for political reasons.

sanctions Measures taken by one state against another to attempt to force a change of policy. Sanctions usually take the form of suspending trade with another country, refusing to buy their goods or to supply them with goods manufactured in any other country.

segregation The practice of creating separate facilities within the same society for another group's use. For example, apartheid in South Africa segregated facilities for whites and blacks.

state of emergency A period during which a government withdraws rights such as freedom of speech in order to limit the possibility of mass violence. A state of emergency is also accompanied by restrictions on movement, such as a curfew during the hours of darkness.

strike A form of industrial action in which workers in a factory or industry stop work to protest about poor working conditions or low pay.

township An area such as a town or city where blacks had to live under apartheid. One such township, Soweto, was the site of the massacre of over 500 protesting students by the South African police in 1976.

treason The crime of attempting to overthrow or damage the government of a country.

United Nations An international organisation formed in 1945 to represent all the governments of the world and to promote peace, cooperation and security between them. The headquarters of the UN is in New York, USA.

vigilante A person who takes upon him or herself the protection of their district or property.

white supremacy A theory or belief that white people are naturally superior to people of other races.

INDEX

ACKNOWLEDGEMENTS

Copyright © ticktock Entertainment Ltd 2003
First published in Great Britain in 2003 by ticktock Media Ltd.,
Unit 2, Orchard Business Centre, North Farm Road, Tunbridge Wells, Kent, TN2 3XF

ISBN 1 86007 423 5 pbk
ISBN 1 86007 430 8 hbk
Printed in Taiwan

We would like to thank: Tall Tree Ltd, Lizzy Bacon and Ed Simkins for their assistance.

10 9 8 7 6 5 4 3 2 1

Picture Credits
Every effort has been made to trace the copyright holders, and we apologize in advance for any unintentional omissions.
We would be pleased to insert the appropriate acknowledgements in any subsequent edition of this publication.

B = bottom; C = centre; L = left; R = right; T = top.
Alamy: 31b, Corbis: 4tl, 7t, 17tr, 20t, 21t, 19b, 23b, 24b, 28-29c, 31r, 32t, 34b, 36b, 41t. Hulton Archive: 13b, 17b, 18l.
Jurgen Schadeberg: 4b, 11t, 12l, 14, 40b. Louise Gubb: 5r, 10b, 21b, 22l, 23c, 24t, 26b, 27cr, 29c, 33b, 37b, 39c, 42t.
PA Photos: 28t, 28b. Topfoto: 30b.